CORPUS OF MAYA

HIEROGLYPHIC INSCRIPTIONS

VOLUME 3   PART 3   YAXCHILAN

CORPUS OF MAYA HIEROGLYPHIC INSCRIPTIONS

Volume 3   Part 3

IAN GRAHAM

Assistant Curator
of Maya Hieroglyphics
Peabody Museum, Harvard University

PEABODY MUSEUM
OF ARCHÆOLOGY AND ETHNOLOGY
HARVARD UNIVERSITY
CAMBRIDGE, MASSACHUSETTS

1982

Distributed by Harvard University Press

ACKNOWLEDGMENTS

Publication of this fascicle was made possible through the generosity of
Mrs. A. Murray Vaughan.

Grateful acknowledgment is made to the Instituto Nacional de Antropología e Historia
of Mexico for their cooperation in authorizing the necessary work at Yaxchilan and for
their permission to reproduce photographs of the sculpture in this the third part of
volume 3. Fieldwork and preparation of the text were carried out under a three-year
grant from the National Endowment for the Humanities and with the benefit of
contributions (matched by the Endowment) from the Bowditch Exploration Fund of
the Peabody Museum and the following generous donors:

The Stella and Charles Guttman Foundation
The Green Foundation
Mrs. Katherine H. Benedict
Mrs. Mary P. Bolles
Judge John L. Clark
Northeastern Pooled Common Fund
The Nonesuch Foundation
Mr. William F. Parady
Mr. Richard D. Wagner

As this book goes to press, the following volumes of the
Corpus of Maya Hieroglyphic Inscriptions are available
from the Harvard University Press, 79 Garden Street,
Cambridge, MA 02138

Yaxchilan, Lintel 59

LOCATION   Found by Linton Satter-
thwaite, Jr., in 1935 in front of the mid-
dle doorway of Structure 24.

CONDITION   Unbroken, though flawed
by a crack through the sculptured edge.
Degree of erosion moderate.

MATERIAL   Limestone.

SHAPE   Parallel-sided.

DIMENSIONS   MW   0.52 m (underside)
             HSc   0.10 m
             WSc   0.65 m
             MTh   0.20 m
             Rel   0.7 cm

CARVED AREAS   One edge only.

PHOTOGRAPH   Graham, 1975.

DRAWING   Graham, based on a drawing
corrected by artificial light and on Satter-
thwaite's 1935 photograph.

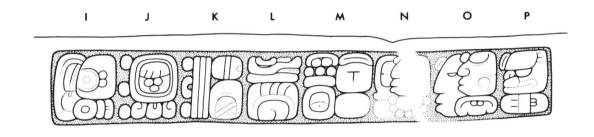

Yaxchilan, Lintel 19

LOCATION   In situ over the doorway in the northwest end of Structure 22, where it was seen by Maler.

CONDITION   Unbroken, but most of the surface that formerly bore an inscription has corroded and scaled away. The portion not thus destroyed retains a hard, almost polished finish with red paint adhering to it.

MATERIAL   Very fine-grained limestone.

SHAPE   The surface is flat; the sides are parallel.

DIMENSIONS
MW	0.65 m	
HSc	0.67 m	(approx.)
WSc	0.52 m	(approx.)
MTh	0.21 m	
Rel	0.1 cm	(approx.)

CARVED AREAS   Underside only, with an incised inscription.

PHOTOGRAPH   Graham, 1978. The lintel having been precariously balanced on a collapsing jamb, and the doorway choked with debris, there was formerly no possibility of photographing it. I am therefore much obliged to Arqueólogo Roberto García Moll for having the jamb consolidated and the doorway cleared out. This doorway proved to have been reduced to about half its original width by a later construction, so that it was still impossible to photograph the entire lower surface of the lintel. Fortunately, the bottom of the panel where glyphs still survive lies over the northeastern and unobstructed side of the doorway. The bottom of glyph A5 is obscured by the jamb.

DRAWING   Graham, based on a tracing made with the use of electric light.

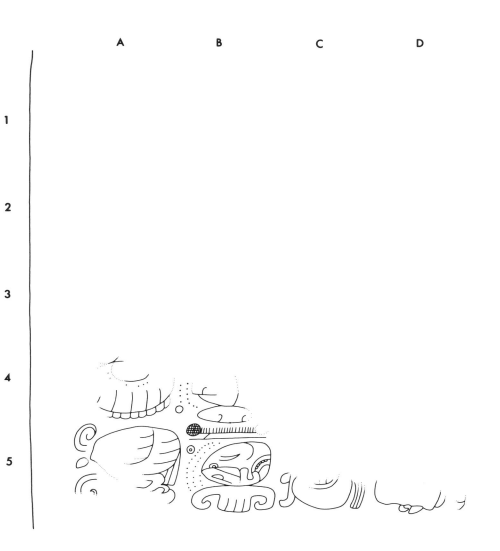

Yaxchilan, Lintel 23

LOCATION   Found during excavation by Roberto García Moll in 1979. The lintel lay among debris in front of the doorway in the western end of Structure 23 that leads into the front chamber. It has since been placed once more over the now reconstructed doorway.

CONDITION   Broken into two pieces. The front edge and rather more than half of the underside are in nearly pristine condition, except for some pitting and unusual erosion cavities that surround the glyph-blocks, the latter perhaps owing their origin to rows of drill holes that may have outlined the raised blocks, as have been noted on a few other sculptures, notably Dos Pilas Stela 8.

MATERIAL   Fine-grained limestone.

SHAPE   A well-formed lintel with parallel sides.

DIMENSIONS   Underside:

MW	0.85 m
HSc	0.86 m
WSc	0.67 m
MTh	0.24 m
Rel	0.9 cm

Front:

HSc	0.16 m
WSc	0.86 m

CARVED AREAS   Underside and front edge.

PHOTOGRAPHS   Graham, 1979.

DRAWINGS   Graham, based on field drawings corrected by artificial light.

REMARKS   I have followed García Moll's suggestion that, as number 23 in Maler's numbering of the lintels came to be unassigned, that number should be assigned to this lintel. Since other lintels from the same structure are numbered 24 to 26, this is perfectly appropriate.

Front, at greater scale

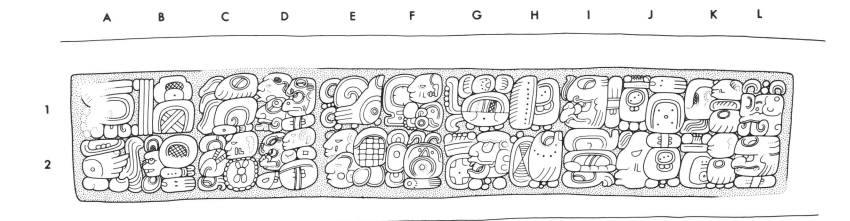

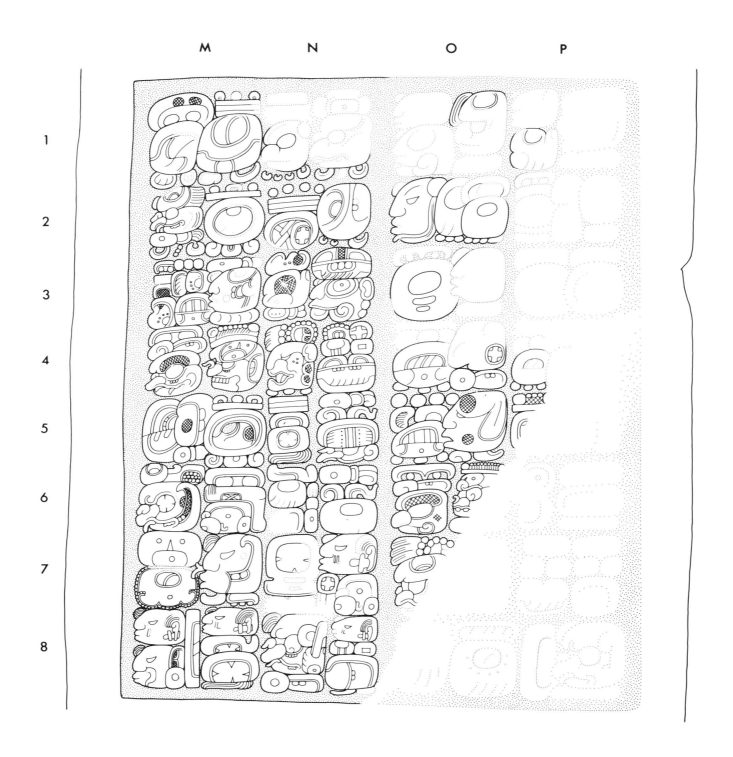

Underside, at greater scale

Additions and Corrections Relating to Yaxchilan Lintels Already Published

Lintel 26

When the drawing published on page 3:57 was in preparation, through oversight no use was made of a plaster cast of the panel containing glyph columns O through R, which is in the Peabody Museum collections. As this cast, made from a wax mold taken by Maler, discloses some mistakes in the published drawing and supplies details missing from it, a new drawing of the glyph panel is presented.

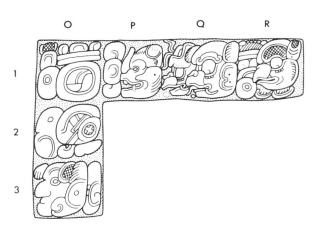

Lintel 34

Subsequent to the publication of this lintel in the second part of this volume, another fragment, undoubtedly one of those mentioned by Morley (see note, p. 3:77), has come to light in the bodega at Yaxchilan. This carries part of glyph D1 and part of D2. The Peabody Museum fragment, tentatively placed in the same position in my drawing and photograph, now seems for textual reasons more likely to have been at B4.

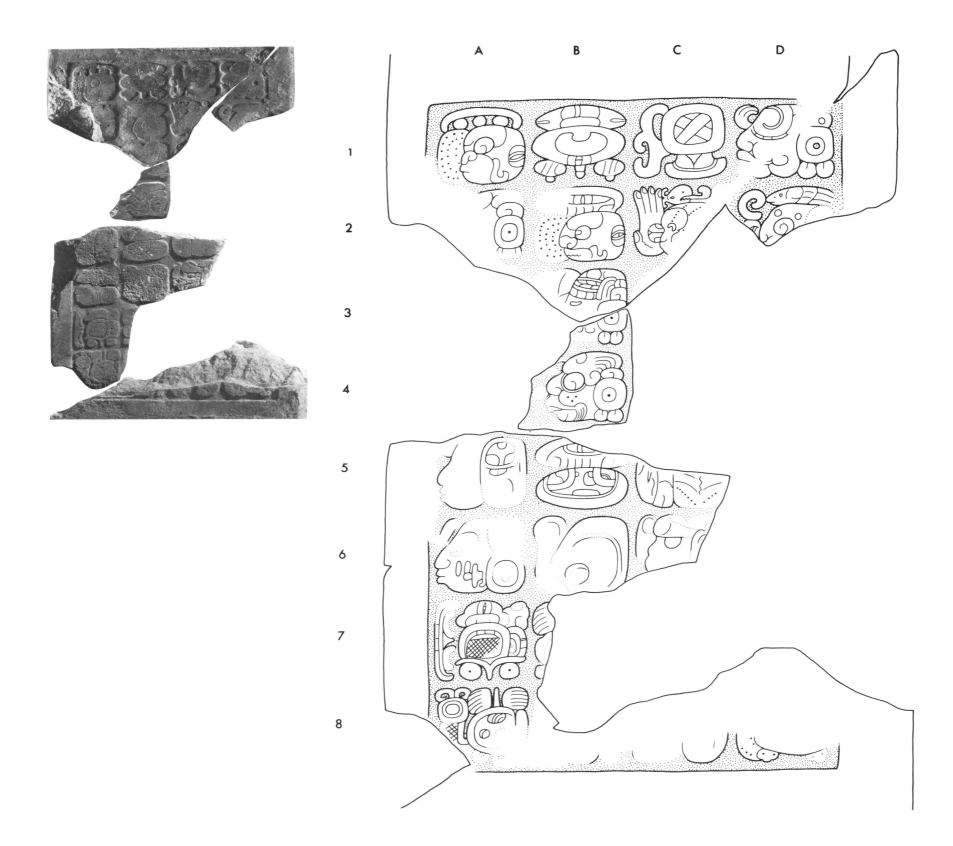

Yaxchilan, Hieroglyphic Stairway 1

NOMENCLATURE The six steps of the stairway are numbered here from top to bottom in Roman numerals I to VI. The blocks within each step are numbered from the left or northern end: I-1, I-2, etc. However, since the inscription runs from block to block as a continuous text uninterrupted by framing borders, and since in many instances part of a particular glyph is carved on one block with the rest of it on the next, the glyphs cannot be assigned letter designations on a block-by-block basis; instead these designations must be applied in a single series for the whole of each step, notwithstanding the uncertainties of doing so in badly weathered passages.

The conventional labeling of glyph-blocks, with letters applied horizontally and numerals vertically, would have involved the use of double and triple primes for this inscription. To avoid such clumsy designations, the glyph-blocks on these steps, as well as those of HS.5, are numbered rather than lettered. In an example of evidently poor planning, the sculptors of this inscription were obliged to introduce a double row of glyphs toward its end. In order to preserve the proper reading order, numerals have been applied to pairs of columns in this section. In accordance with Morley's practice, the left and right columns of such pairs can be distinguished by the addition of the letters *a* and *b* to the glyph-block number and the upper and lower halves by the addition of *u.h.* and *l.h.* Reference to such a glyph may therefore take this form: YAX:HS.1,83*b*,*l.h.*

LOCATION The lower steps of the stairway were discovered by Maler, the upper steps remaining obscured by debris until cleared by members of the Carnegie Institution expedition of 1931. The stairway is part of Structure 5, a platform of some size constructed on the river bank, with its rear overlooking the seasonally submerged "masonry pier" and its front forming the central element of the northeastern side of the largest plaza at Yaxchilan. The Hieroglyphic Stairway provides access to the platform from this plaza.

CONDITION Most of the 111 blocks forming this stairway remain in position, or have been only slightly disturbed. One block (VI-2) has fallen forward and now lies beneath the roots of a tree. A few are broken into several pieces, and many have had one or two pieces broken from them. (Some of these we were able to re-store to their original position for photography.) Unfortunately, the general condition of the sculptured risers is deplorable, much of the stone having become very soft.

MATERIAL Limestone. Three of the blocks (I-9, IV-7, and V-13) are set with their bedding planes vertical and perpendicular to the plane of the risers.

DIMENSIONS Step I is 13.55 m long; the lengths of the others lie between 13.75 and 13.90 m. The widths of the treads, ascending from Step VI to Step II, are 0.90, 1.00, 0.80, 0.65, and 0.65 m.

CARVED AREAS Risers only. Study of the large cartouches, especially that on Block I-17, raises the possibility that they may have been carved over the original text.

PHOTOGRAPHS The entire stairway was photographed by Graham step by step in 1970, and again with better lighting in 1980. Unfortunately, some of the latter series were ruined during development. The published photographs are taken from both series.

DRAWINGS Graham, based on field drawings corrected by artificial light.

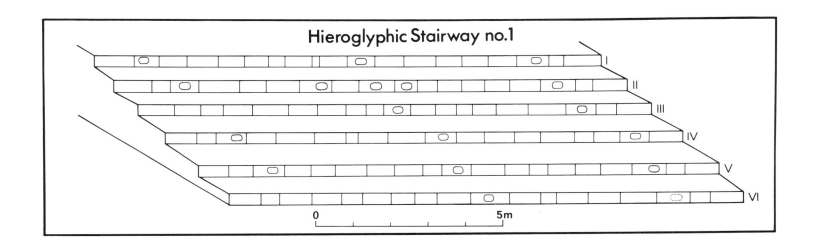

Hieroglyphic Stairway no.1

Step I

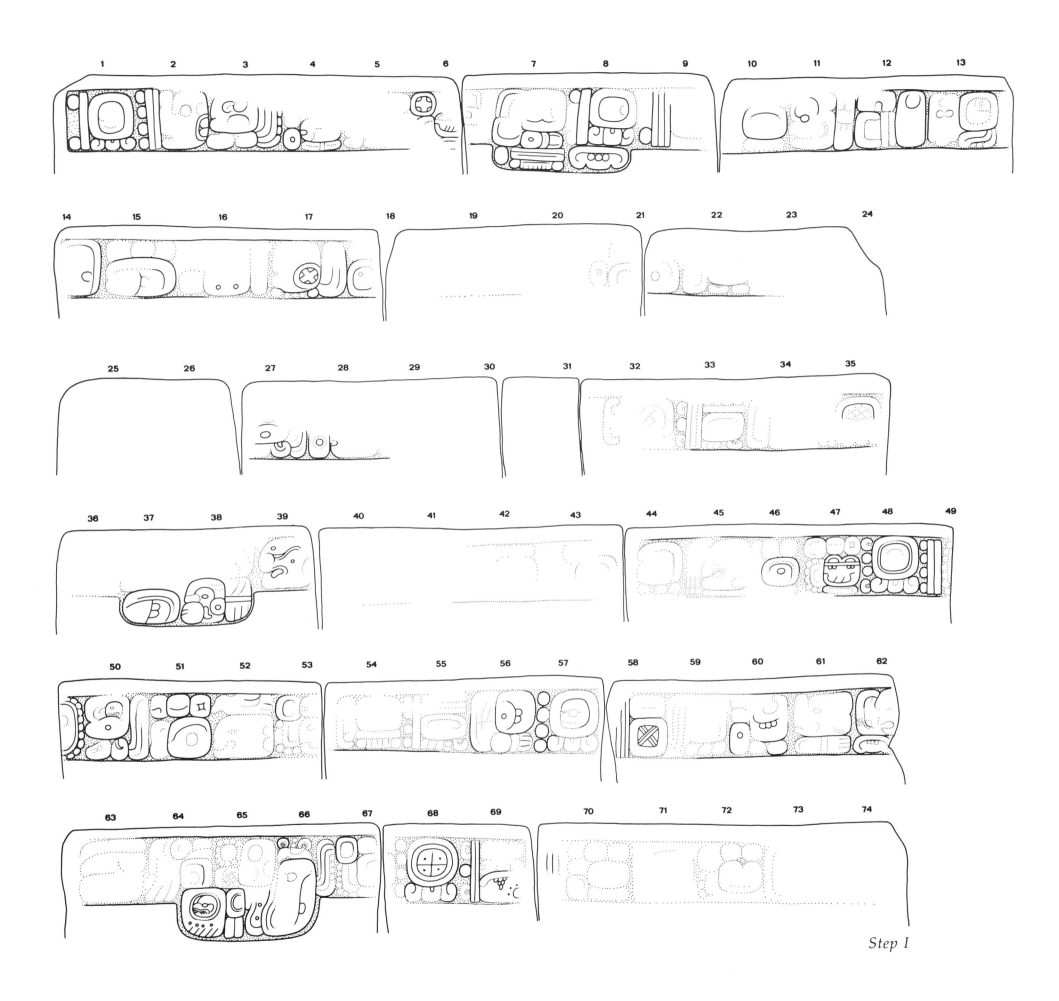

Step I

Step II

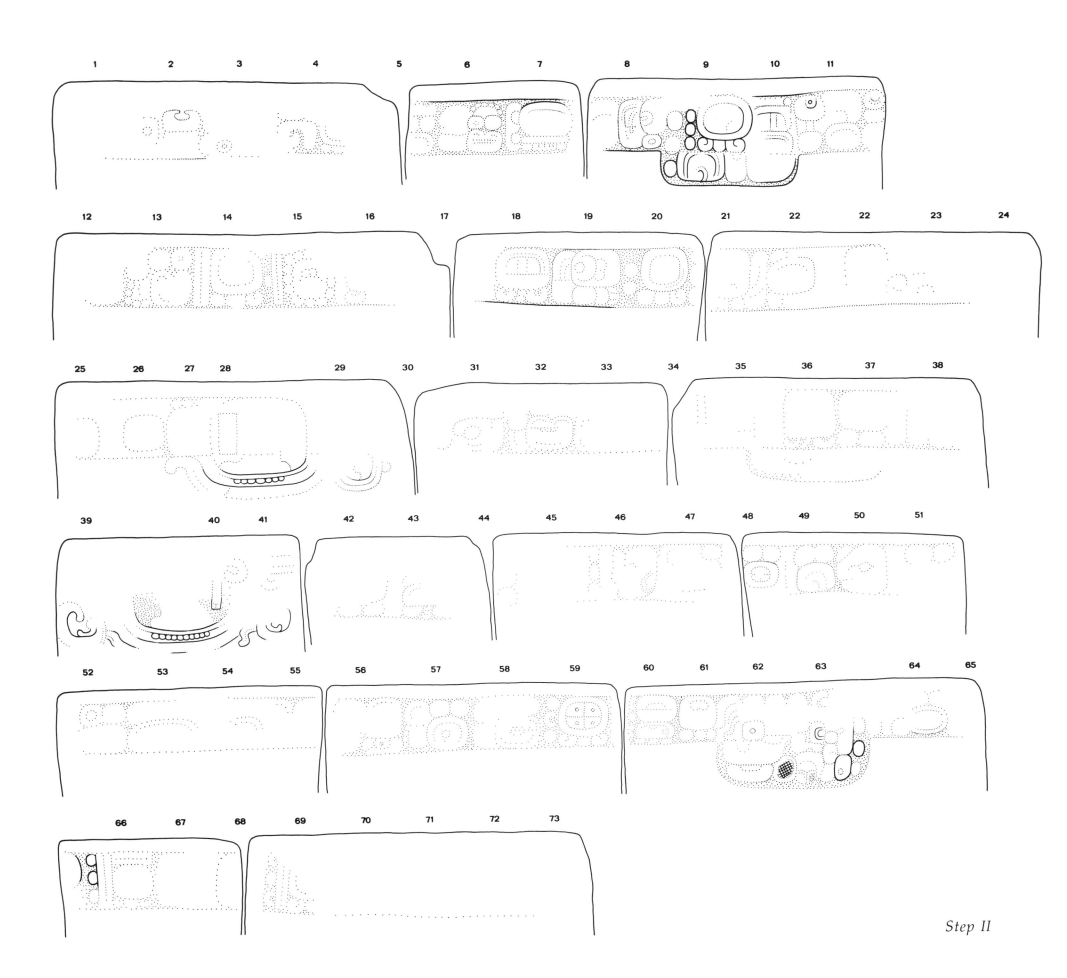

Step II

Step III

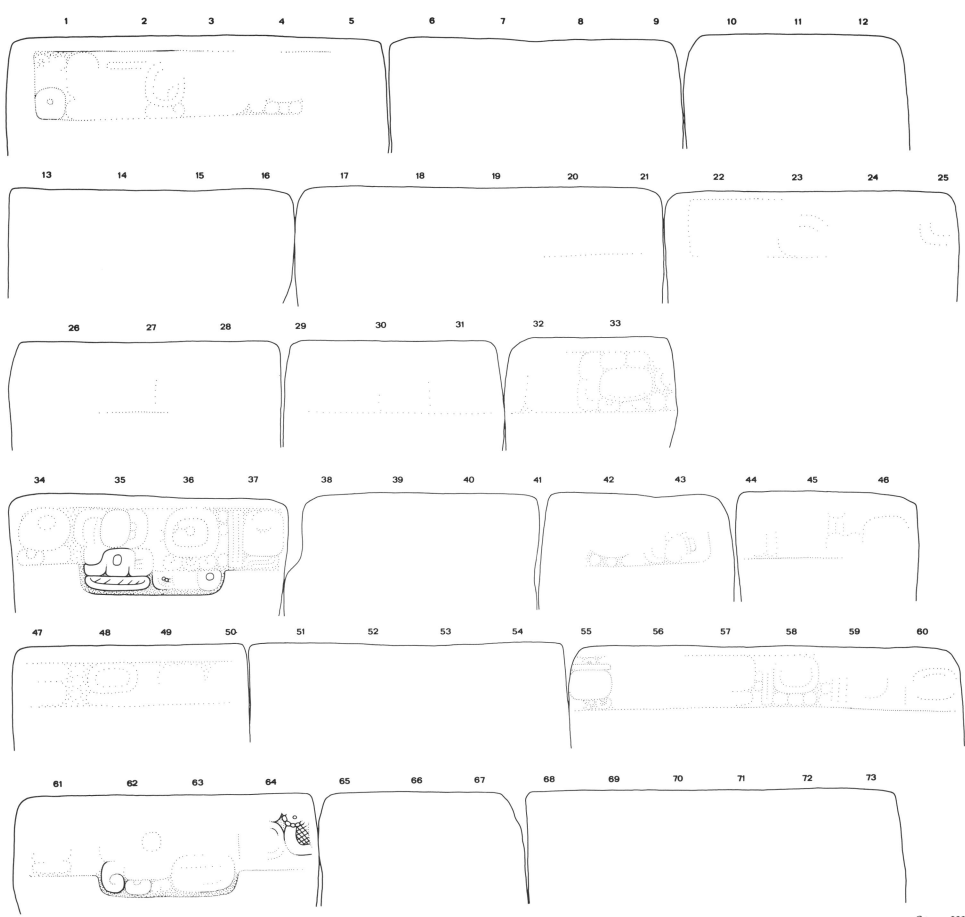

Step III

Step IV

Step IV

Step V

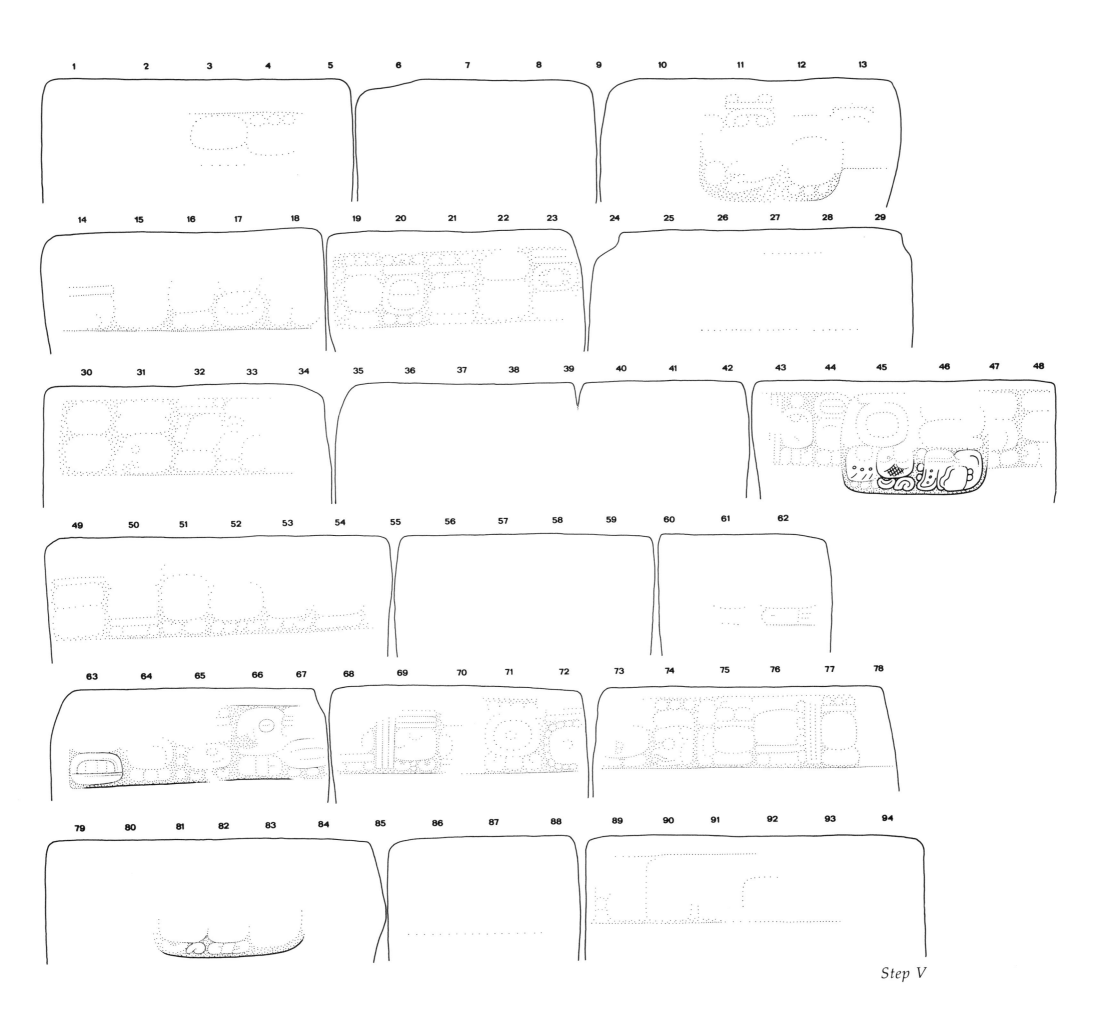

Step V

Step VI

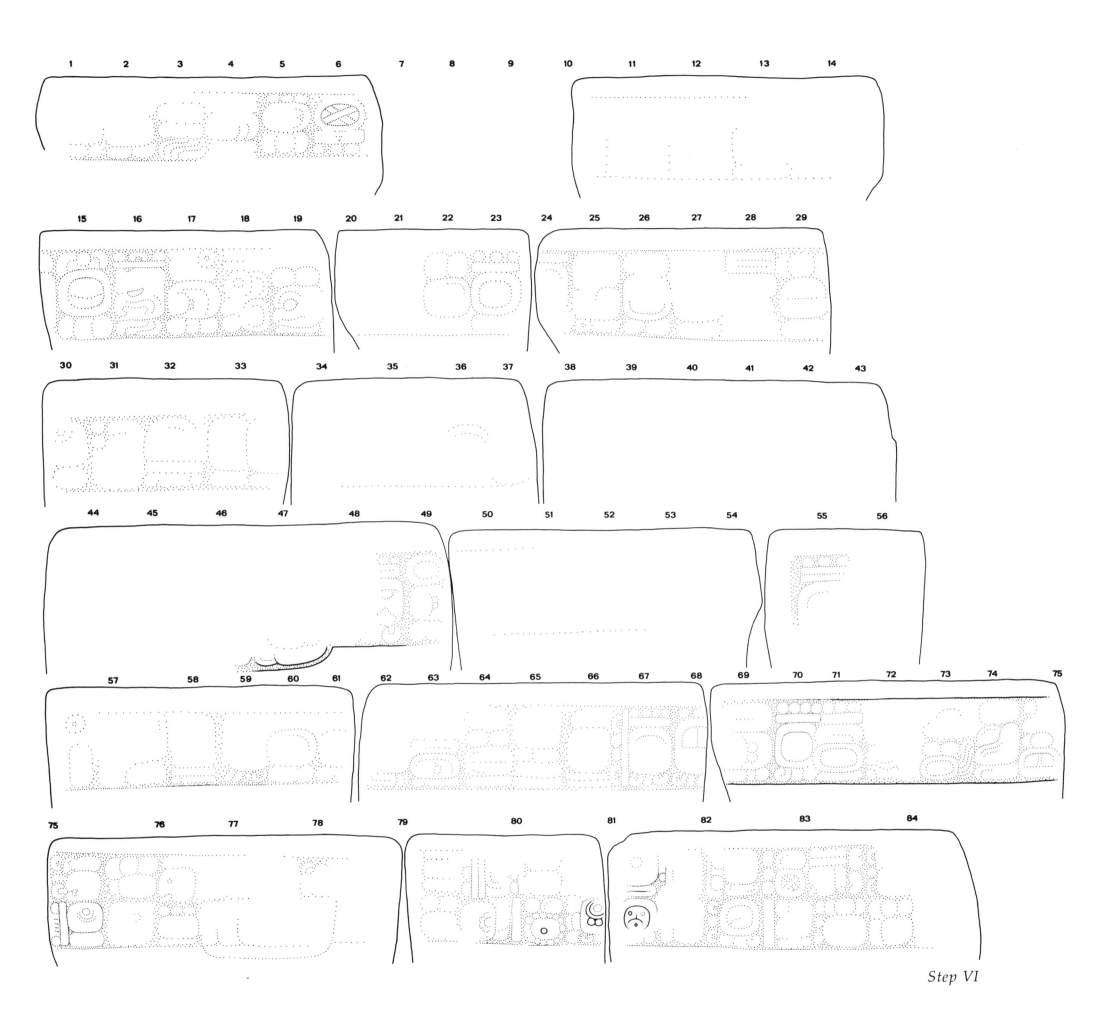

Step VI

Yaxchilan, Hieroglyphic Stairway 2

NOMENCLATURE The blocks constituting this step are numbered in Roman numerals I to XIII. Individual hieroglyphs may be referred to in this form: YAX:HS.2-VII,A1.

LOCATION The step was discovered by Roberto García Moll in 1975 during his program of clearing and consolidating Structure 33. The step is the last in the long ascent to this temple, and it runs nearly the full width of the building. The thirteen carved blocks extend slightly beyond the two outer doorways of the temple, the step itself continuing in both directions with uncarved and less massive blocks. (See the sketch plan on this page. This has been drawn to include Stela 31, the incised stalactite, in order to remedy the incorrect position given it in the site plan, pp. 3:6,7.)

CONDITION As found, the three central blocks, VI to VIII, were in a nearly pristine state. In common with the others they have suffered some damage to their upper edges from falling masonry. The other blocks (of clearly different style and origin) were more weathered, some of them being almost obliterated. The only block from which a substantial portion is missing is Block IV.

MATERIAL Limestone, of various qualities. The three central blocks are of yellowish stone of uniform fine grain.

SHAPE Most of the blocks are well trimmed, with dressed treads, although they lack depth below the carved area such as is commonly found in the sculptured steps of the Maya.

CARVED AREAS Risers only.

PHOTOGRAPHS Graham, 1975.

DRAWINGS Graham, based on field drawings corrected by artificial light.

DIMENSIONS

Block	Ht	MW	HSc	WSc	Rel (cm)
I	0.40	0.77	0.27	0.60	1.0
II	0.42	0.96	0.30	0.77	0.2
III	0.42	0.86	0.32	0.72	0.5
IV	0.35	0.80*	0.26	—	0.2
V	0.32	0.87	0.26	0.69	0.2
VI	unknown	0.81	0.35	0.70	3.5
VII	unknown	1.65	0.38	1.53	4.0
VIII	unknown	0.97	0.33	0.84	3.0
IX	0.56	1.10	0.30	0.81	0.2
X	0.36	0.88	0.25	0.69	0.2
XI	0.38	0.75	0.27†	—	0.3
XII	0.36	0.68	0.26	0.52	0.2
XIII	0.36	0.85	0.28†	0.65†	incised

*estimated original width
†approximate

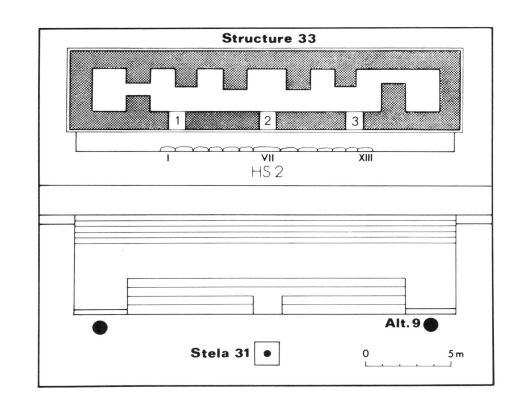

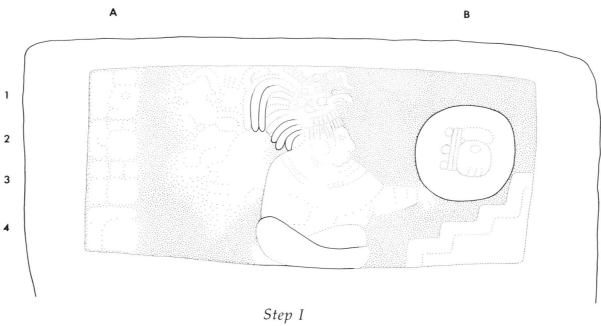

Step I

Step II

A   B   C   D   E   F   G   H   I

Step III

A   B   C   D

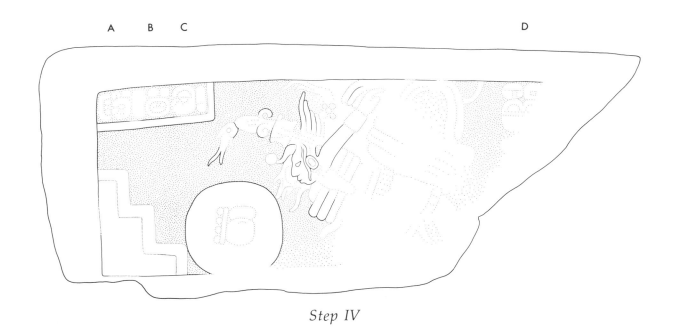

Step IV

A B C

1

2

3

Step V

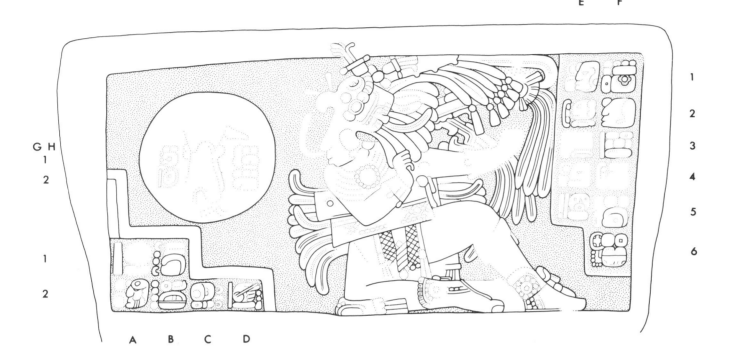

Step VI   *Detail*

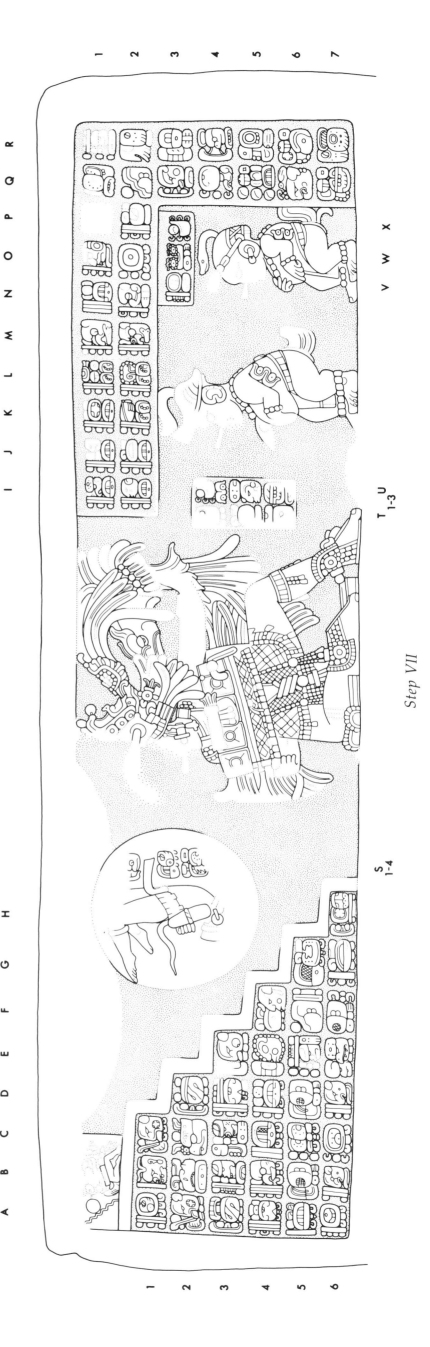

Step VII

Detail

Detail

Detail

Step VIII

Detail

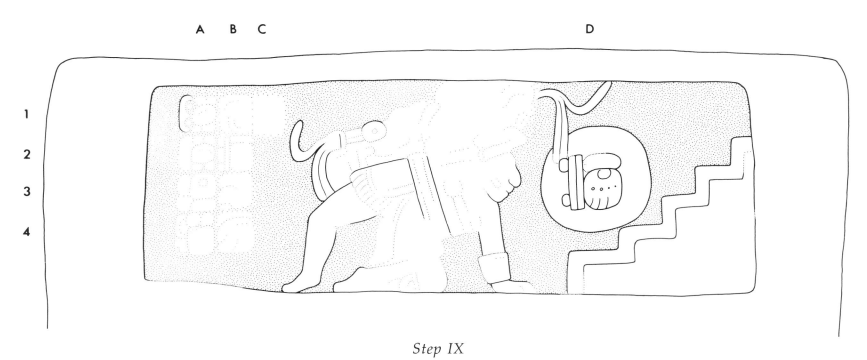

Step IX

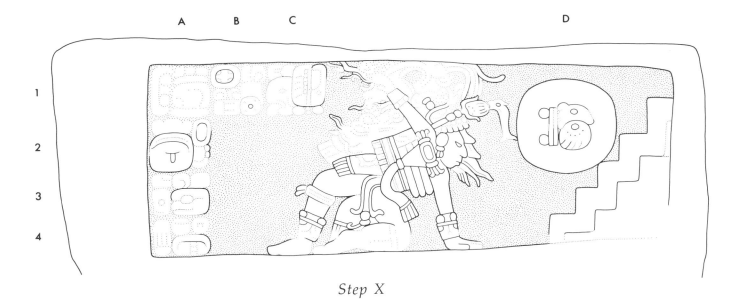

Step X

YAX: HS. 2

3:164

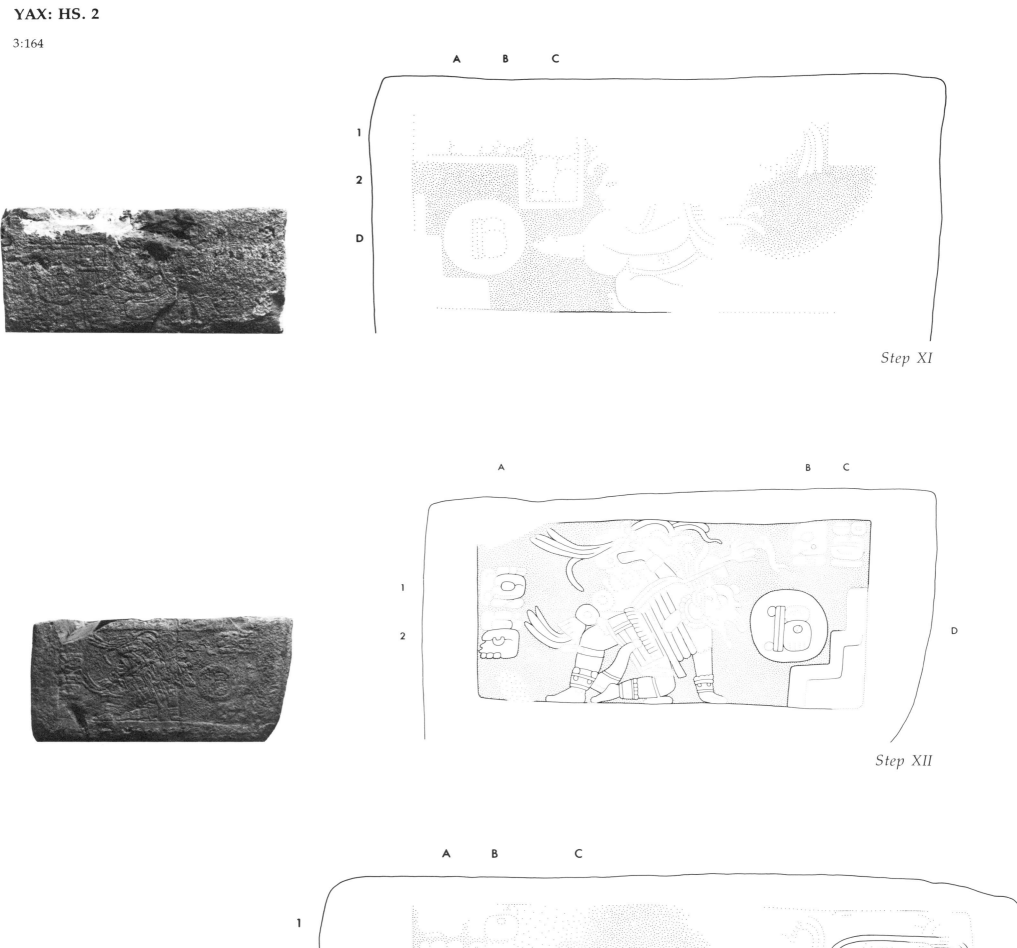

Step XI

Step XII

Step XIII

Yaxchilan, Hieroglyphic Stairway 3

NOMENCLATURE The hieroglyphic stairway is made up of pairs of inscribed steps giving access to each of the three doorways of Structure 44. The six blocks are numbered here in Roman numerals I to VI, passing from upper to lower step and from southeastern to northwestern doorway, i.e., from the doorway of Lintel 44 to that of Lintel 46. Individual hieroglyphs may be referred to in this form: YAX:HS.3–VI,A1. See the note below for concordance between Morley's designation of glyph-blocks and that employed here.

LOCATION Block III was discovered in 1900 by Maler, although it was not recognized by him as a step. Its true nature became clear in 1931 when Karl Ruppert of the Carnegie Institution cleared the doorways and discovered the other five blocks of the stairway. All of them were in place, whereas Block III had at some time in the past been pulled out and left lying upside down near the edge of the terrace.

All three upper steps are considerably wider than the doorways in front of which they were set: Block I has a sculptured tread 1.53 m wide, whereas the doorway is only 1.06 m wide. At some time after the steps had been put in place, and perhaps in response to fears for the stability of the building, a reinforcing wall 30 cm thick was built along the front wall of the building, with openings corresponding exactly with the original doorways. This wall obscured nearly half the width of those parts of the sculptured area of each upper step that extended beyond the doorjambs on either side. I am much indebted to Roberto García Moll for consenting in 1979 to have the relevant portions of the wall dismantled in order to reveal the hidden areas of sculpture. In passing, it may be mentioned that Morley was mistaken in stating that these areas were covered when the doorway was *narrowed* (Morley 1937–38, vol. 2, pp. 448, 452). It is noteworthy that this wall remains intact on both sides of the central doorway; this means that Block III had already been removed from its presumed original setting when this wall was built.

The five steps found in situ by Ruppert remain where found, but not Block III; it has disappeared. Perhaps it was removed in 1964 when other pieces were being taken to the Museo Nacional de Antropología and was lost during the journey upstream to Agua Azul, or at some other stage. Most unfortunately no photograph seems to exist of the riser, which Maler mentions as having been carved with eight double glyph-blocks.

CONDITION All six blocks were intact when found. The treads of the upper steps were in good condition; the risers still extant have suffered significant loss through erosion and fracture and are obscured in places by deposits of lime. Of the lower steps, Block IV is well preserved; the other two are badly weathered.

DIMENSIONS

Treads:	I	II	III	IV	V	VI
Ht	1.65*	1.46	1.98	over 1.80	1.61	1.43
MW	0.72	0.75	0.75	0.70	0.71	0.78
HSc	1.53	1.29	†	1.20	1.52	1.34
WSc	0.60	0.61	†	0.58	0.60	0.70
Rel	1.0 cm	1.5 cm	†	0.9 cm	1.0 cm	1.5 cm

Risers:						
Ht	0.30			0.30		0.32
HSc	0.22			†		0.18
WSc	1.49			†		1.47

*approximate
†no record
(all dimensions in meters except where specified)

MATERIAL Limestone.

SHAPE The upper steps were worked into impressive rectangularity; the lower, which were to be set into the plaster floor of the terrace, are less regular in outline.

CARVED AREAS Blocks I, III, V: tread and riser. Blocks II, IV, VI: tread only.

PHOTOGRAPHS Graham, 1976 and 1979, except for the photograph of Block III, which is Maler's (printed from a copy negative, the original being lost).

DRAWINGS Graham, based on field drawings corrected by artificial light, except for the drawing of Block III, which is based on Maler's and Morley's photographs.

NOTES 1. Calculation indicates a uinal coefficient of 2 in the Distance Number at A5 on Block I, but one dot and two fillers are shown. However, the relief of the crescent fillers is shallower than in the rest of the inscription, and the dot is scarcely perceptible. This suggests the possibility of an attempt having been made to correct the mistake, with the crescents perhaps being filled in with plaster.

2. Morley designated the glyph columns on the lintels and steps of Structure 44 as a single series running from A to J″. His scheme is presented graphically in *The Inscriptions of Peten* (Morley 1937–38, vol. 2, fig. 27). In the present work each block of the stairway is lettered separately. The following is a concordance between Morley's lettering (cited first) and that employed here:

Block I	V	A	Block II	F′	A
	W	B		G′	B
	X	C		H′	C
	Y	D		I′	D
	Z	F,G		J′	C
	A′	H,I		K′	—
	B′	J,K			
	C′	L,M			
	D′	N,O			
	E′	P,Q			

Block III	A	A	Block IV	M	A
	B	B		N	A
	C	C		O	B
	D	D		P	B
	E	F,G		Q	C
	F	H,I			
	G	J,K			
	H	L,M			
	I	N,O			
	J	P,Q			
	K	R,S			
	L	T,U			

Block V	M′	A	Block VI	W′	A
	N′	B		X′	B
	O′	C		Y′	C
	P′	D		Z′	D
	Q′	F,G			
	R′	H,I			
	S′	J,K			
	T′	L,M			
	U′	N,O			
	V′	P,Q			

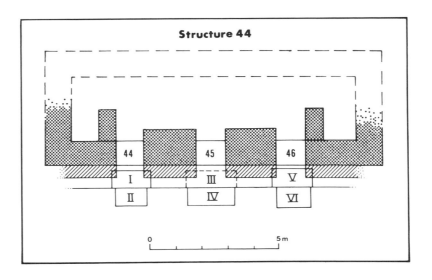

Structure 44

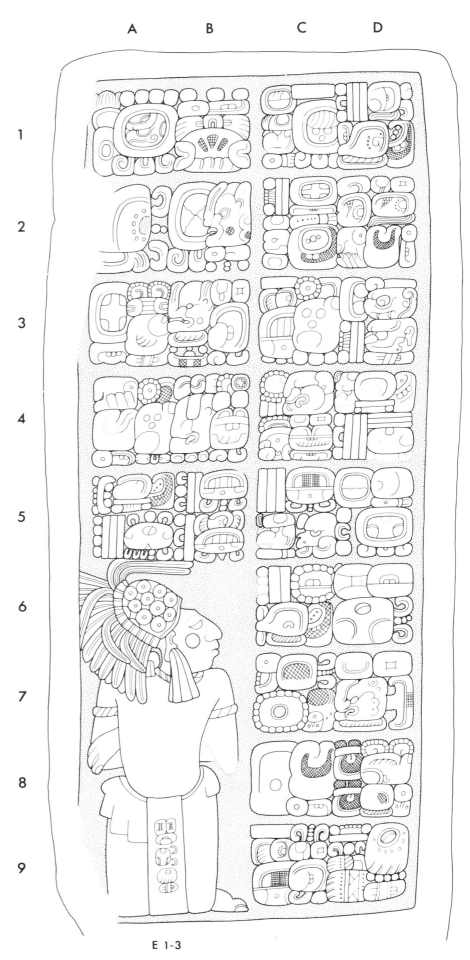

E 1-3

Step I Tread

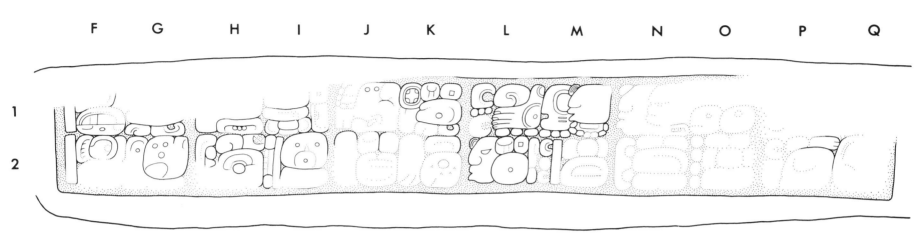

Step I   Riser

Step II

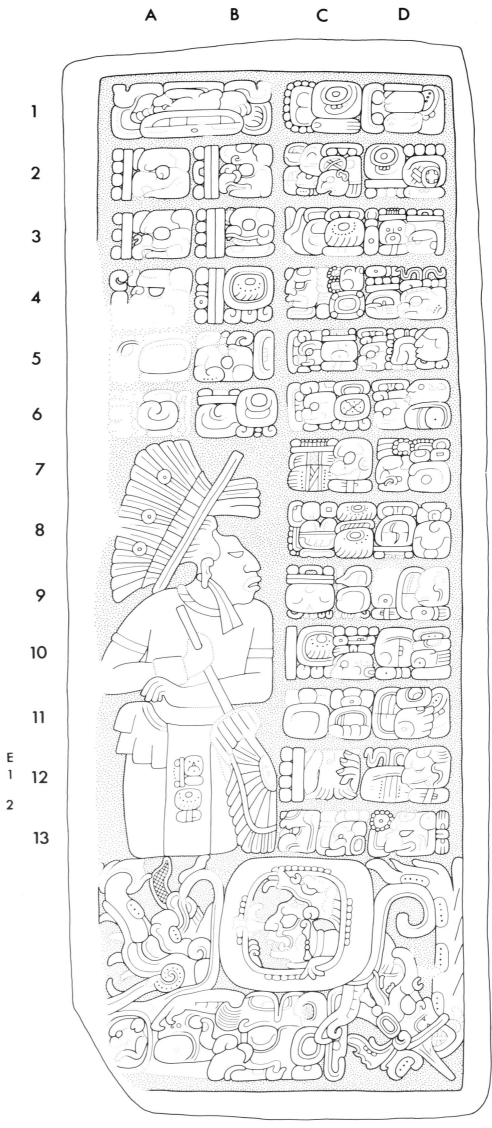

Step III

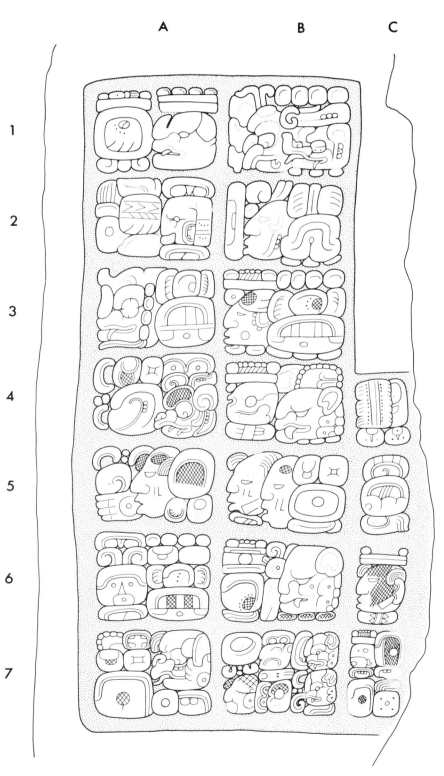

Step IV

E 1-3

Step V   *Tread*

F G H I J K L M N O P Q

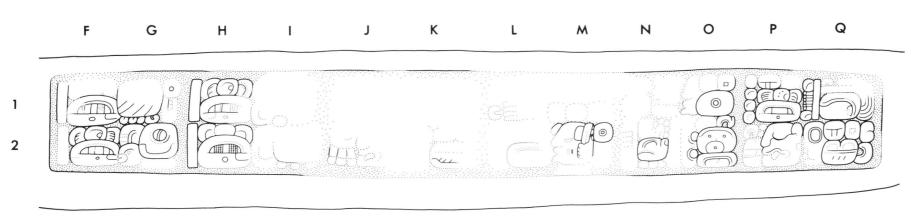

1

2

Step V   Riser

Step VI

Yaxchilan, Hieroglyphic Stairway 4

NOMENCLATURE The three inscribed blocks are numbered in Roman numerals I to III from southeast to northwest, that is, left to right. Individual hieroglyphs may be referred to in this form: YAX:HS.4-3,B1.

LOCATION The steps were discovered in 1980 by Roberto García Moll in the course of clearing and consolidating Structure 41. The three inscribed blocks are set into a step that runs the full width of the building, each step being set directly in front of one of the doorways.

CONDITION Block I: part of the carved surface carrying Column D of the inscription and a fragment carrying the central portion of the Introducing Glyph have split off, only the latter having come to light. Erosion varies from moderate to serious in different areas of the surface. Block II: broken into three or four pieces, only two of which have survived. Erosion of the surface has rendered the inscription illegible. Block III: intact and moderately well preserved.

DIMENSIONS

	Block I	Block II	Block III
Ht	1.20 m	0.89 m	1.40 m
MW	0.50 m	0.58 m	0.72 m
HSc	1.01 m		1.05 m
WSc	0.38 m plus		0.44 m
MTh	0.08 m	0.16 m	0.18 m
Rel	0.4 cm		0.9 cm

MATERIAL Limestone of grayish color with, in the case of Block I, a pronounced laminar texture.

SHAPE Block III is well fashioned; the other two may have resembled it.

CARVED AREAS Tread only.

PHOTOGRAPHS Graham, 1980.

DRAWINGS Graham, based on field drawings corrected by artificial light.

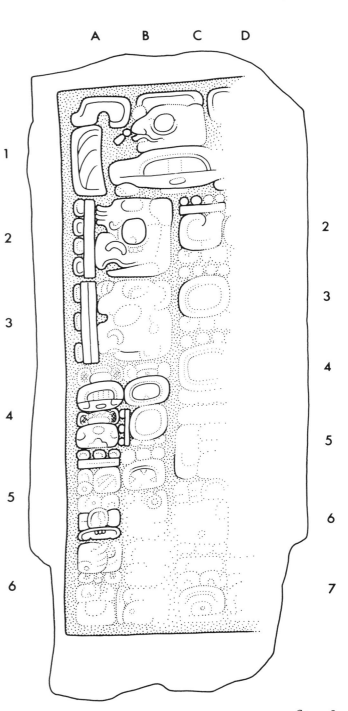

Step I

Step II

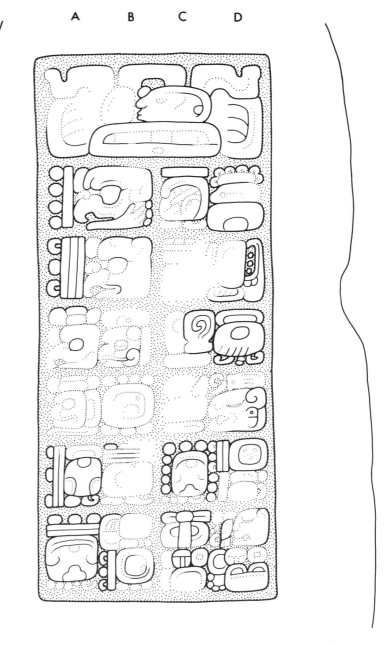

Step III

Yaxchilan, Hieroglyphic Stairway 5

NOMENCLATURE The stone blocks constituting the step are numbered 1 through 45 without regard to the missing blocks that evidently preceded number 1 at the southeast end. However, in numbering the glyph-blocks the lost section has been taken into consideration by starting the numeration at 36, a number reckoned large enough to include the glyph-blocks now missing. In view of this, strict adherence to the usage recommended in the *Introduction* (p. 1:11, note 2) requires that glyph-block designations in this step be prefixed by *p*, for provisional. The suggested form for referring to a particular glyph is thus: YAX:HS.5,p152.

Two blocks both carved with hieroglyphs in two rows were found close to the step and so are likely to have borne some relation to it in their original setting; they have therefore been designated HS.5a and HS.5b.

LOCATION The step runs across the front, or northeast side, of Structure 20, 1.80 m from the facade and about 5 m from the edge of the terrace. The step also serves two flanking buildings not yet excavated at the time of writing, the one to the southeast being only a low mound. For some reason all of the blocks that formed the step in front of this flanking mound have decayed, some to the point of disappearance. Proof that they too were inscribed, however, is provided by the outline of a cartouche on one block. The two blocks, HS.5a and HS.5b, were found lying in debris, one above and one below the step, near the gap between Stones 22 and 25.

The existence of the step was unknown until the temple was cleared of debris by Roberto García Moll in 1980, prior to consolidation of the masonry.

CONDITION As mentioned above, the first part of the inscription, some 6 m long, is completely destroyed. The next part, that lying in front of Structure 20 proper, has suffered serious fracturing in places from the impact of stones falling from the high facade. There are also three gaps in this stretch. Beyond the temple no serious damage is seen, and the inscription remains in good condition, having been covered by slump from the northwest flanking mound (which may lie closer to the step than is shown in the sketch plan).

MATERIAL Limestone.

SHAPE Well-trimmed rectangular blocks. The depth of stone below the lower edge of the inscription runs up to 0.30 m. Block 18, set in front of the central doorway, is much wider (1.61 m) than the others.

CARVED AREAS Risers only.

PHOTOGRAPHS Graham, 1981.

DRAWINGS Graham, based on complete stereophotographic coverage.

DIMENSIONS

	Blocks 1–45:		
	HSc	0.18	m average
	Rel	0.9	cm
	Total length 29.20 m		
	Step height above plaster line approx. 0.30 m		
HS.5a:	MW	0.42	m
	WSc	0.38	m
	Ht	0.39	m
	HSc	0.28	m
	Rel	0.7	cm
HS.5b:	MW	0.34	m
	WSc	0.30	m
	Ht	0.39	m
	HSc	0.28	m

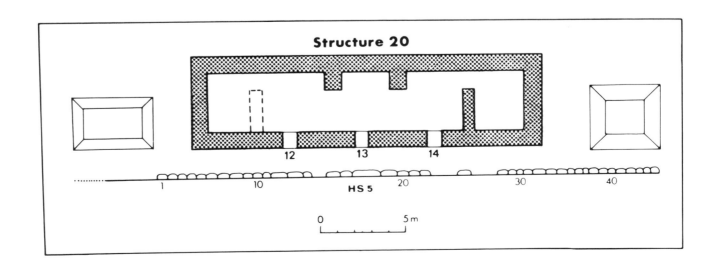

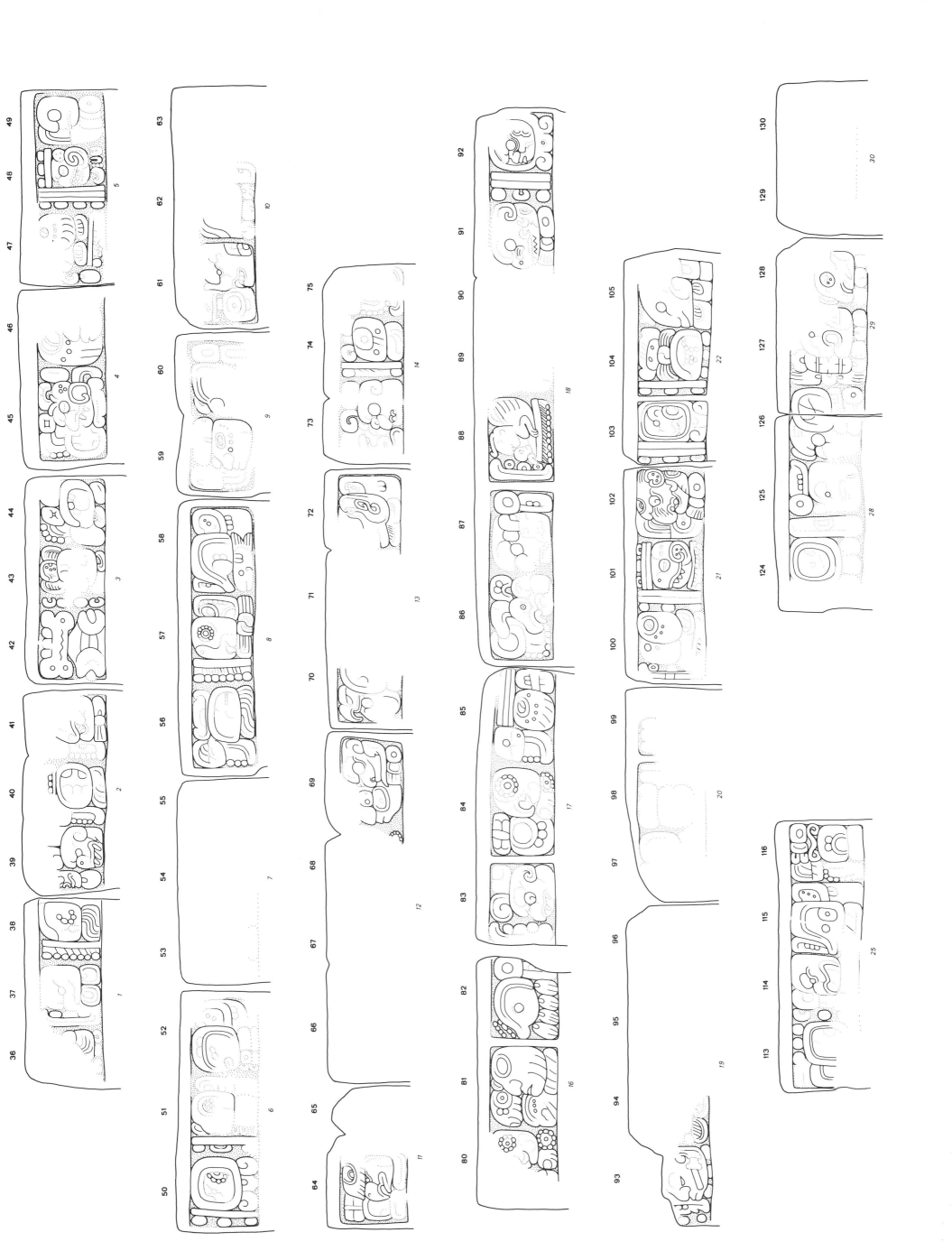

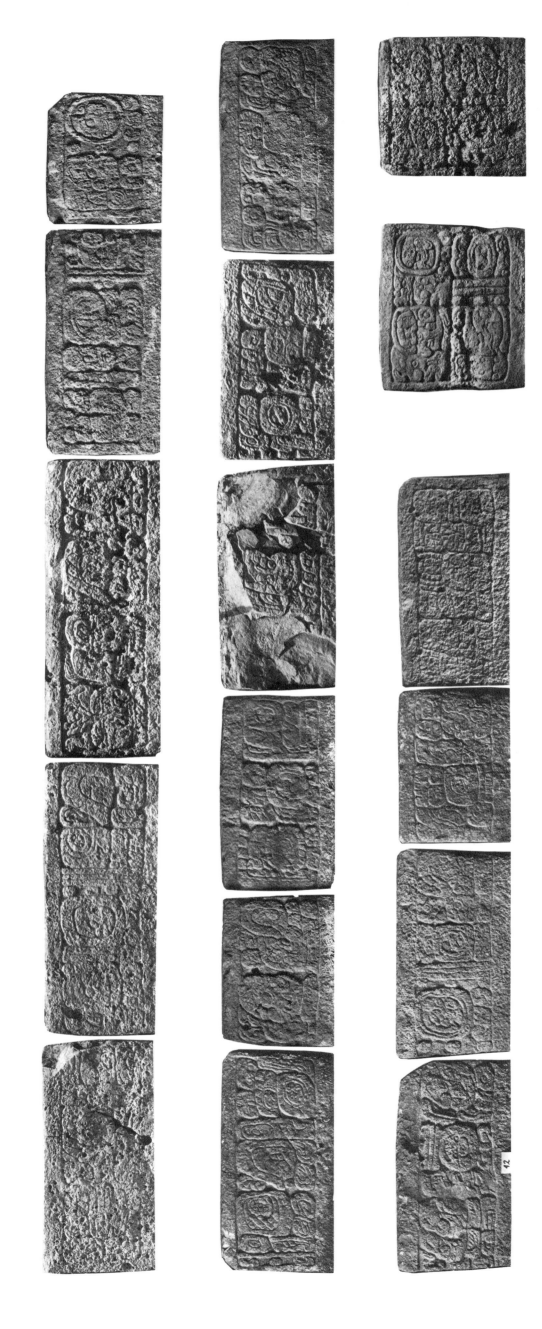

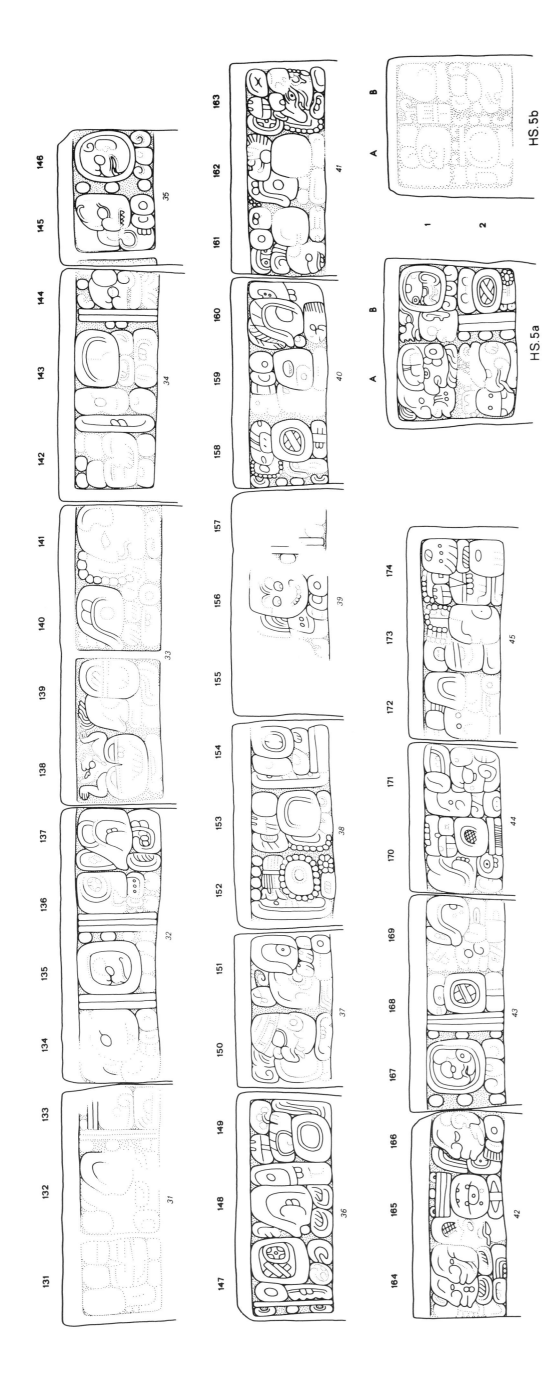

Map of the Maya Area

In 1974 when the *Introduction* to this work was being written, it was thought that publication of a map designed to show the location of Maya sites would be premature, simply because so few of them could be placed with sufficient accuracy (p. 1:10). An additional difficulty that was not mentioned lay in the lack at that time of adequate base maps for the Mexican and Belizean portions of the area.

With the passage of six years the situation has improved. Complete coverage of Belize in maps at the scale of 1:50 000 is now available, and there is hope of equivalent maps of Chiapas and the Yucatan Peninsula becoming available in the foreseeable future. In the central lowlands the location of many sites has now been established with enough accuracy (or so we hope) to justify the publication of a sheet covering that area.

The scale of 1:500 000 that has been adopted allows the area within which virtually all Maya sites lie to be covered in seven sheets of convenient size, the coverage of each sheet being shown in the key on this page. With this fascicle, then, comes the Central Lowlands sheet (to be found in the back cover pocket); other sheets will be issued from time to time as will revised editions of sheets already published, when these become necessary.

A number of sites lacking inscriptions have been marked on the map, their inclusion being somewhat arbitrary, although size was an important criterion. Smaller sites of which we have knowledge will be shown, in due course, on the 1:125 000 maps published in this work with each site described because of its inscriptions.

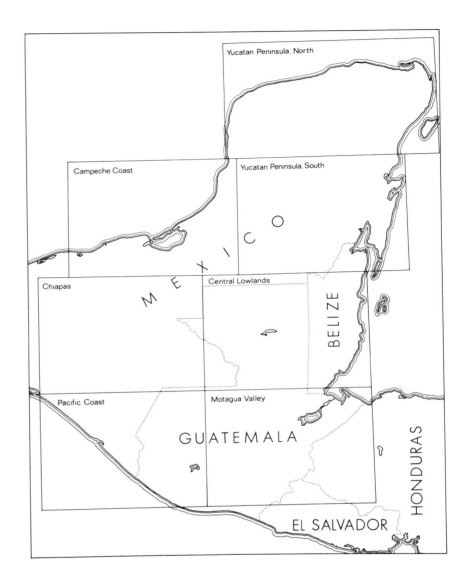

Sources of Sculpture and Their Codes

Sites

Abaj Takalik   ABJ
Acanmul   ACN
Acte   ATE
Actuncan   ATU
Aguas Calientes   AGC
Aguateca   AGT
Almuchil   AMC
Altamira   ALM
Altar de Sacrificios   ALS
Altun Ha   ALH
Amelia, La   AML
Amparo, El   AMP
Anonal   ANL
Arroyo de Piedra   ARP
Balakbal   BLK
Balamtun   BLM
Baúl, El   BUL
Becan   BCN
Bejucal   BJC
Benque Viejo, see Xunantunich
Bonampak   BPK
Calakmul   CLK
Campeche   CMP
Cancuen   CNC
Cansacbe   CNS
Caracol   CRC
Caribe, El   CRB
Cayo, El   CAY
Cedral, El   CDR
Ceibal, see Seibal
Cenotillo   CNT
Chacchoben   CHB
Chal, El   CHL
Chalchuapa   CLC
Chapayal   CPL
Chiapa de Corzo   CPC
Chichen Itza   CHN
Chichmul   CMU
Chicozapote, El   CZP
Chilib   CLB
Chinaha   CNH
Chinikiha   CNK
Chinkultic   CKL
Chochkitam   CKM
Chocola   CCL
Chorro, El (Peten)   CRO
Chuctiepa   CTP
Chumuc-ha, see Pusilha
Chunhuitz   CNZ
Cival   CVL
Coba   COB
Collections, public or private   COL
Comalcalco   CML
Comitan   CMT
Consacbe   CSB
Copan   CPN
Corozal   CRZ
Cozumel   COZ
Dos Pilas   DPL
Dos Pozos, see Dos Pilas
Dzehkabtun   DZK
Dzibilchaltun   DBC
Dzibilnocac   DBN
Dzilam   DZL
Dzitbalche   DZT
Edzna, see Etzna
Ek Balam   EKB
Encanto, El (Chiapas), see Finca Encanto
Encanto, El (Peten)   ENC
Esperanza, La   ESP
Etzna   ETZ

Finca Encanto   FNC
Flores   FLS
Florida, La   FLD
Guaquitepec   GQT
Guaymil, see Uaymil
Hacienda Tabi, see Tabi
Halakal   HLK
Halal   HLL
Haltunchon   HLT
Hatzcab Ceel, see Mountain Cow
Higos, Los   HIG
Holactun, see Xcalumkin
Honradez, La   HRZ
Hotzuc, Hacienda   HTZ
Huacutal   HUA
Huntichmul   HNT
Ichmac   ICC
Ichmul   ICL
Ichpaatun   ICP
Iki, see Ikil
Ikil   IKL
Itsimte-Sacluk   ITS
Itzan   ITN
Itzimte-Bolonchen   ITB
Ixkun   IXK
Ixlu   IXL
Ixtelha   IXH
Ixtutz   IXZ
Izapa   IZP
Jaina   JAI
Jimbal   JMB
Jonuta   JNT
Kabah   KAB
Kaminaljuyu   KJU
Kana   KNA
Kanki   KNK
Kaxuinic   KAX
Kayal   KYL
Kumche, see Ichmul
Kuna, see Lacanha
Labna   LAB
Lacanha   LAC
Laguna Perdida   LGP
Lagunita   LAG
Lashtunich   LTI
Loltun   LOL
López Mateos   LPM
Lubaantun   LBT
Macanxoc, see Coba
Machaquila   MQL
Managua   MNG
Mar, La   MAR
Mario Ancona   MNC
Maxcanu   MXC
Mayapan   MPN
Menche, see Yaxchilan
Milpa, La   MLP
Mirador   MRD
Miraflores   MRF
Montura, La   MTR
Mopila   MPL
Moral   MRL
Morales, see Moral
Motul de San José   MTL
Mountain Cow   MCW
Mulchic   MLC
Muluch Seca, see Muluch Tsekal
Muluch Tsekal   MLS
Muñeca, La   MCA
Naachtun   NCT
Na Balum Winik, see Lacanha

Najtunich   NTN
Nakum   NKM
Naranjo   NAR
Naya, La   NAY
Nimli Punit   NMP
Nohoch Mul, see Coba
Nohpat   NPT
Ojo de Agua   OAG
Okop   OKP
Oxkintok   OXK
Oxlahuntun   OXL
Oxpemul   OXP
Pabellón, El   PAB
Padre Piedra   PDR
Pajaral   PJR
Palenque   PAL
Palmar, El   PLM
Panhale   PNH
Pantaleón   PNT
Paraíso, El (Yucatan)   PRS
Pasadita, La   PSD
Pasión del Cristo   PCR
Pato, El   PAT
Pechal   PCL
Peru, El   PRU
Pestac   PST
Pich Corralche, see Xcoralche
Pie de Gallo   PDG
Piedra Labrada   PLB
Piedras Negras   PNG
Pixoy   PIX
Pochitoca, La   PCT
Poco Uinic, see Santa Elena P.U.
Polol   POL
Pomona, Belize   PMB
Pomona, Tabasco   PMT
Pomuch   PMC
Portón, El   PRT
Porvenir, El   PVR
Pusilha   PUS
Quen Santo, see Sacchana
Quirigua   QRG
Retiro, El   RTR
Río Amarillo   RAM
Río Azul   RAZ
Río Bec   RBC
Río Michol   RMC
Sacchana   SCN
Sacnicte   SNT
Sacul   SCU
San Diego   SDG
Salinas de los Nueve Cerros   SAL
San Clemente   SCM
San Isidro Piedra Parada, see
   Abaj Takalik
San Lorenzo, Campeche   SLM
San Lorenzo, Chiapas   SLS
San Pedro, see Dzitbalche
Santa Elena Poco Uinic   SEP
Santa Margarita Colomba, see
   Abaj Takalik
Santa Rita Corozal   SRC
Santa Rosa Xlabpak, see Santa
   Rosa Xtampak
Santa Rosa Xtampak   SRX
Santoton   STN
Sayil   SAY
Seibal   SBL
Silan, see Dzilam
Simojovel   SMJ
Sisilha   SIS

Codes

PJR	Pajaral		XCR	Xcoralche
PLB	Piedra Labrada		XCS	X'Castillo
PLM	El Palmar		XKB	Xkombec
PMB	Pomona, Belize		XKM	Xkichmook
PMC	Pomuch		XLM	Xcalumkin
PMT	Pomona, Tabasco		XMK	Xmakabatun
PNG	Piedras Negras		XNC	Xnucbec
PNH	Panhale		XNH	Xnaheb
PNT	Pantaleón		XTL	Xutilha
POL	Polol		XUL	Xultun
PRS	El Paraíso, Yucatan		XUN	Xunantunich
PRT	El Portón		XUP	Xupa
PRU	El Peru		YAX	Yaxchilan
PSD	La Pasadita		YLC	Yalcabakal
PST	Pestac		YLT	Yaltutu
PUS	Pusilha		YUL	Yula
PVR	El Porvenir		YXH	Yaxha
QRG	Quirigua		YXM	Yaaxhom
RAM	Río Amarillo		YXN	Yaxuna
RAZ	Río Azul		YXP	Yaxcopoil
RBC	Río Bec		ZAP	El Zapote
RMC	Río Michol		ZPB	Zapote Bobal
RSB	Resbalón		ZPT	Zacpeten
RTR	El Retiro		ZTZ	El Zotz
SAL	Salinas de los Nueve Cerros			
SAY	Sayil			
SBL	Seibal			
SCM	San Clemente			
SCN	Sacchana			
SCU	Sacul			
SDG	San Diego			
SEP	Santa Elena Poco Uinic			
SIS	Sisilha			
SLM	San Lorenzo, Campeche			
SLS	San Lorenzo, Chiapas			
SMJ	Simojovel			
SNT	Sacnicte			
SRC	Santa Rita Corozal			
SRX	Santa Rosa Xtampak			
STN	Santoton			
SUF	La Sufricaya			
TAM	Tamarindito			
TBI	Tabi			
TCH	Techoh			
TCK	Tohcok			
TIK	Tikal			
TLA	Tila			
TLT	Telantunich			
TMB	El Temblor			
TMN	Teleman			
TNA	Tonina			
TNL	Tonala			
TNP	Tenam Puente			
TNR	Tenam Rosario			
TPX	Topoxte			
TRS	Tres Islas			
TRT	El Tortuguero			
TSL	Tayasal			
TUL	Tulum			
TUN	Tunkuyi			
TZB	Tzibanche			
TZC	Tzocchen			
TZD	Tzendales			
TZM	Tzum			
UAX	Uaxactun			
UCN	Ucanal			
UKM	Ukum			
UOL	Uolantun			
UXL	Uxul			
UYM	Uaymil			
XCA	Xcocha			
XCK	Xcochkax			
XCL	Xculoc			

Index to Volumes 1 to 3